He[illegible] Diet Recipes

The Collection

Jacqueline Whitehart

Healthy Diet Recipes

York

www.52recipes.co.uk

A catalogue record for this book is available from the British Library.

ISBN: 978-1546597681

This book features weight-loss techniques which may not be suitable for everyone. You should always consult with a qualified medical practitioner before starting any weight-loss programme, or if you have any concerns about your health. This book is not tailored to individual requirements or needs and its contents are solely for general information purposes. It should not be taken as professional or medical advice or diagnosis. The activities detailed in this book should not be used as a substitute for any treatment or medication prescribed or recommended to you by a medical practitioner. The author and the publishers do not accept any responsibility for any adverse effects that may occur as a result of the use of the suggestions or information herein. If you feel that you are experiencing adverse effects after embarking on any weight-loss programme, including the type described in this book, it is imperative that you seek medical advice. Results may vary from individual to individual.

Book One

Book Two

Book Three

Healthy Diet Recipes

CHICKEN

Fresh, Healthy and Easy Recipes
from best-selling cookery author,
Jacqueline Whitehart.

Healthy Diet Recipes: Chicken

Healthy Diet Recipes: Chicken

This new set of easy diet recipes are designed to be easy to follow, quick recipes that you can with little fuss. I love cooking for myself and my family but often find that cookbooks tend towards the 'special' or 'weekend' recipes whereas what we want 99% of the time is something simple and healthy that we can make from scratch and avoid the dreaded processed or ready meals. All the recipes are carefully crafted to be well-balanced and healthy and are calorie-counted for your convenience. Most if not all recipes can be kept or frozen in individual portions to provide several days worth of healthy meals.

For people following healthy diets, we all know chicken is simply the best in terms of filling protein, low fats and deliciousness. Chicken is endlessly versatile and lends itself well to a weeknight dinner for a couple or family. By adding different flavours with herbs and spices we can create a huge array of dishes so you'll never get bored.

MEDITERRANEAN CHICKEN WITH FETA

259 calories

Serves 2 • Ready in 45 minutes

2 × 150g (5oz) skinless, boneless chicken breasts (318 cals)

1 tbsp tomato purée (paste) (30 cals)

1 tsp chopped fresh basil

1 tsp olive oil (27 cals)

1 garlic clove, peeled and finely sliced (3 cals)

1 × 400g (14oz) can whole tomatoes (64 cals)

a pinch of salt

1 tbsp red wine vinegar (1 cal)

25g (1oz) light feta cheese, cut into small cubes (75 cals)

- Cut each chicken breast into 2 pieces and lightly score on both sides. Rub the tomato purée (paste) and half the basil over the 4 pieces of chicken and leave to rest while you prepare the sauce.
- Heat the olive oil gently in a non-stick saucepan, add the garlic and fry for 1–2 minutes until just starting to brown. Add the canned tomatoes, salt and the remaining basil and simmer over a medium heat for 10 minutes. Reduce the heat and break up the tomatoes with the back of a wooden spoon. Add the red wine vinegar and continue to simmer gently for another 10 minutes.
- Meanwhile, preheat the grill to medium. Arrange the chicken pieces on the grill pan and grill for 7–8 minutes on each side. The chicken should be cooked through and turning golden all over.
- Add the chicken and feta to the tomato sauce and stir in. Heat for a further 2–3 minutes, then serve.

HONEY MUSTARD CHICKEN SKEWERS

200 calories

The chicken in this dish is very tender and delicious. If using wooden skewers, make sure they are soaked in a bowl of water for at least 30 minutes before using to prevent them burning during cooking.

Serves 1 • Ready in 20 minutes

2 tsp wholegrain mustard (14 cals)

1 tsp runny honey (23 cals)

grated zest and juice of 1 lime (4 cals)

1 × 150g (5oz) skinless, boneless chicken breast, cut into 6 small pieces (159 cals)

- Mix the mustard, honey, lime zest and juice and 1 tablespoon water together in a bowl. Add the chicken and stir until the chicken pieces are coated all over with the marinade. You could cook the chicken straight away but it tastes much better if it is left to marinate for about 30 minutes in the refrigerator.
- Preheat the grill to medium. Thread the chicken pieces onto skewers. You want 2 short skewers with 3 pieces of chicken on each, leaving room between the chicken pieces to allow them to cook thoroughly.
- Place the chicken skewers on a grill pan and grill for 6–8 minutes on each side. Check that the chicken is cooked through and chargrilled all over before serving.

CHINESE CHICKEN STIR-FRY

306 calories

The slightly strange marinade for the chicken really works and gives the dish a Chinese takeaway feel.

Serves 2 • Ready in 30 minutes (including marinade time)

1 small egg white (7 cals)

2 tsp cornflour (cornstarch) (36 cals)

2 × 150g (5oz) skinless chicken breasts, cut into strips (318 cals)

1 tsp Thai fish sauce (nam pla) (4 cals)

juice of 1 lime (4 cals)

1 tsp vegetable oil (27 cals)

½ red (bell) pepper, deseeded and cut into large chunks (27 cals)

2.5cm (1in) piece of fresh ginger, peeled and grated (20 cals)

1 shallot, peeled and thinly sliced (6 cals)

1 garlic clove, peeled and thinly sliced (3 cals)

1 red chilli, deseeded and sliced (2 cals)

300g (11oz) bag mixed vegetable stir-fry (158 cals)

8 fresh basil leaves

- Whisk together the egg white and 1 teaspoon of cornflour (cornstarch) with a fork. Tip in the chicken and stir to coat. Leave to marinate for 10 minutes if you can.
- Remove the chicken from the marinade and pat dry with kitchen paper (paper towels).
- Combine the fish sauce, lime juice, 2 tablespoons water and the rest of the cornflour.
- Heat the oil in a wok or wide heavy-based frying pan (skillet) over

a medium–high heat. When hot, toss in the chicken and stir-fry for 4–6 minutes until just cooked. Remove the chicken from the pan.

- Turn the heat to maximum and stir-fry the (bell) pepper, ginger, shallot, garlic and chilli for 2 minutes. Add the bagged veg and stir-fry for another 2 minutes until tender. Pour in the fish sauce mix and add the chicken and basil leaves. Heat through and serve immediately.

GARLIC GRILLED CHICKEN

187 calories

This dish is marinated in a milky sauce, giving it a wonderful succulence.

I have given a recommended marinating time of 30 minutes but it is even better if left for an hour or even overnight in the fridge.

Serves 2 • Ready in 20 minutes plus 30 minutes marinade

100ml (½ cup) buttermilk (47 cals)

2 garlic cloves, peeled and crushed (6 cals)

salt and freshly ground black pepper

2 × 150g (5oz) skinless chicken breasts (318 cals)

- Stir the garlic and salt and pepper into the buttermilk.
- Lightly score the chicken breasts, then place in a wide bowl and pour the milk over. Turn the chicken in the sauce to make sure it is fully covered. Cover the bowl with clingfilm, then chill for at least 30 minutes.
- When you are ready to cook the chicken, heat the grill to a medium-high setting. Remove the chicken from the marinade and place on a grill pan. When the grill has reached the correct temperature, grill the chicken for 7–10 minutes on each side until cooked through.

PAPRIKA CHICKEN SALAD

300 calories

One of my favourite easy salads, the chicken is very tender when quick fried in this way.

Serves 1 • Ready in 15 minutes

1 × 150g (5oz) skinless chicken breast, cut into 4–5 slices (159 cals)

½ level tbsp plain (all-purpose) flour (34 cals)

salt and freshly ground black pepper

½ tsp paprika (3 cals)

1 tsp olive oil (27 cals)

100g (3½oz) bag baby leaf salad (21 cals)

100g (3½oz) cucumber (about 5cm/2in piece), roughly chopped (10 cals)

10 cherry tomatoes, halved (22 cals)

1 tbsp low-fat natural yogurt (22 cals)

¼ tsp paprika (2 cals)

- Place the chicken in a bowl and sprinkle on the flour, salt and pepper and ½ teaspoon paprika. Use your hands to toss the chicken in the flour and make sure it is evenly covered.
- Heat the oil in a frying pan (skillet) over a medium heat. When hot, add the chicken and fry for about 4 minutes on each side, depending on thickness.
- Meanwhile, prepare all your salad ingredients and place in a serving bowl. Combine the yogurt and ¼ teaspoon paprika in a small cup.
- Place the just cooked chicken on top of the salad and drizzle the yogurt dressing over.

CHICKEN POACHED IN WHITE WINE

322 calories

Yes! This is as good as it sounds.

Serves 1 • Ready in 20 minutes

1 tsp olive oil (27 cals)

½ garlic clove, peeled & crushed (2 cals)

2 spring onions, trimmed & sliced (10cals)

½ tsp dried mixed herbs

1 × 150g (5oz) skinless chicken breast, halved (159 cals)

100ml (½ cup) dry white wine (66 cals)

1 tbsp light soft cheese (25 cals)

small handful of fresh parsley (10g), chopped (3 cals)

- Heat the oil, garlic, spring onions (scallions) and dried mixed herbs in a small lidded frying pan (skillet) or saucepan for 1–2 minutes until sizzling. Add the chicken and cook for about 4 minutes until the first side turns golden.
- Turn the chicken over and add the white wine. Put the lid on and turn the heat to low. Let the chicken continue to cook in the wine for a further 5 minutes. Check that the chicken is cooked through before removing from the pan and covering.
- Bring the remaining liquid in the pan back up to simmering and stir in the soft cheese. Bubble for 2–3 minutes until you get a pleasingly thick sauce. Stir in the parsley and pour over the chicken.

CORIANDER AND LEMON CHICKEN

199 calories

This chicken dish is incredibly fresh and tasty. Serve with new potatoes and a zingy salad.

Serves 1 • Ready in 15 minutes + 1 hour marinade time

1 × 150g (5oz) skinless, boneless chicken breast, cut in half and lightly scored (159 cals)

½ lemon (8 cals)

½ garlic clove, peeled and crushed (2 cals)

1 handful of fresh coriander (cilantro) leaves, chopped (4 cals)

1 tsp olive oil (27 cals)

salt and freshly ground black pepper

- Put the chicken into the marinade and use your fingers to rub the marinade all over until the chicken is coated. Cover and leave to rest in the refrigerator for at least 1 hour.
- Wash the lemon in hot soapy water (only if waxed) and dry on kitchen paper (paper towels). Using the fine side of the grater, grate a little of the zest of the lemon into a medium-sized bowl. Add the garlic, coriander (cilantro) leaves, olive oil and the juice of the ½ lemon. Mix together with a little salt and pepper.
- Heat a griddle pan or frying pan (skillet) over a medium-high heat. Add the chicken, press it into the pan and cook for about 6–8 minutes on each side, turning the heat down if it looks like it's starting to catch, until the chicken is cooked through. Leave to rest in the pan for 2 minutes before serving.

YIN AND YANG CHICKEN SALAD

211 calories

This Asian-style salad should keep you going through the day.

Serves 2 • Ready in 15 minutes

220g (7½oz) skinless, boneless chicken breast, cut into strips (233 cals)

½ onion, peeled and roughly chopped (27 cals)

1 bay leaf

1 stalk lemongrass, bruised with the back of a knife

For the salad:

10cm (4in) cucumber, peeled (10 cals)

a pinch of salt

1 celery stick, cut into thin strips (5 cals)

1 medium carrot, peeled and cut into long, thin strips (35 cals)

80g (3¼oz) white cabbage, thinly shredded (22 cals)

1 small handful of fresh coriander (cilantro) leaves, roughly chopped (3 cals)

1 small handful of fresh mint leaves, roughly chopped (6 cals)

2 tsp sesame seeds (60 cals)

6 little gem lettuce leaves (3 cals)

For the dressing:

½ garlic clove, peeled & crushed (2 cals)

½ small red chilli, deseeded and cut into rings (1 cal)

½ tsp granulated sugar (10 cals)

juice of 1 lime (4 cals)

1 tsp fish sauce (1 cal)

- Place the chicken in a lidded saucepan and add the onion, bay leaf and lemongrass. Cover with water and bring to the boil. Put the lid on the pan, reduce the heat and simmer for 10–12 minutes or until the chicken is cooked. Remove the chicken from the pan with a slotted spoon and leave to cool.
- For the salad, using a vegetable peeler, cut the cucumber into flat strips. Discard the seeds, then place on a large plate and sprinkle with the salt. Set aside for 10 minutes.
- Meanwhile, make the dressing by placing all the dressing ingredients in a small bowl, adding 1 tablespoon water and mixing together.
- Squeeze the excess water out of the cucumber, then place in a large bowl and add the celery, carrot, cabbage and herbs. Mix in the cooked chicken and half the sesame seeds, then stir in the dressing.
- Arrange the lettuce leaves on 2 serving plates, then pile the salad on top of the lettuce and sprinkle with the remaining sesame seeds. Serve.

GRILLED CHICKEN TOPPED WITH SUN-DRIED TOMATOES AND OLIVES

293 calories

If you can't find rocket salad try a mixed leaf salad instead.

Serves 1 • Ready in 20 minutes

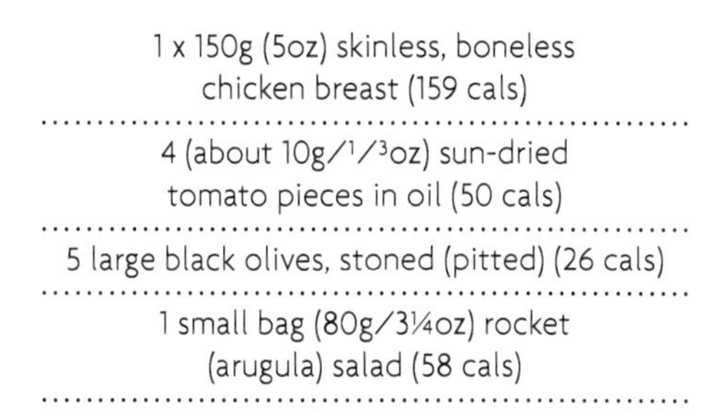
1 x 150g (5oz) skinless, boneless chicken breast (159 cals)

4 (about 10g/1/3oz) sun-dried tomato pieces in oil (50 cals)

5 large black olives, stoned (pitted) (26 cals)

1 small bag (80g/3¼oz) rocket (arugula) salad (58 cals)

- Preheat the grill (broiler) to medium-high.
- Cut the chicken into 2 pieces and lightly score it on both sides. Place in a bowl. Roughly chop the tomato and black olives and add to the bowl. Press the mixture into the scores on the chicken and rub any remaining bits over the top.
- Put the chicken on the grill pan and grill (broil) for 7–8 minutes on each side. Check that the chicken is cooked all the way through.
- Arrange the rocket (arugula) salad on a serving plate, put the chicken on top and serve.

CHILLI CHICKEN SALAD

274 calories

This chicken is marinated for an hour to make it beautifully tender when cooked.

Serves 1 • Ready in 15 minutes + 1 hour to marinade

2 spring onions (scallions), trimmed and finely chopped (9 cals)

2 garlic cloves, peeled and finely chopped (6 cals)

juice of 1 lemon (4 cals)

½ tsp honey (47 cals)

½ tsp paprika (3 cals)

¼ tsp mild chilli powder

salt and freshly ground black pepper

1 × 150g (5oz) chicken breast fillet, cut into 8 pieces (159 cals)

For the salad:

¼ iceberg lettuce, shredded (14 cals)

5cm/2in piece cucumber, diced (10 cals)

2 vine-ripened tomatoes, diced (20 cals)

juice of ½ lemon (2 cals)

- First, make a marinade by combining the spring onions (scallions), garlic, lemon juice, honey, spices and a little salt and pepper in a bowl. Add the chicken pieces to the bowl. Cover and leave to marinate in the refrigerator for about 1 hour.
- When you are ready to cook the chicken, preheat the grill to medium. Place the chicken pieces on the grill pan and grill for 8–10 minutes, turning once. They should be brown and crispy all over and the chicken cooked through.
- Place the lettuce, cucumber and tomatoes in a serving bowl and arrange the chicken over the top. Mix the lemon juice with salt & pepper to make a dressing and pour over the top. Serve immediately.

ONE POT LEMON CHICKEN

395 calories

This dish has a very appetizing lemon colour.

Serves 4 • Ready in 30 minutes

1 lemon

1 tsp olive oil (27 cals)

4 × 150g (5oz) skinless chicken breasts (636 cals)

1 red onion, peeled and cut into wedges (54 cals)

2 tsp medium curry powder (14 cals)

1 tsp turmeric

200g (1 cup) basmati rice (718 cals)

500ml (generous 2 cups) hot chicken stock

(made with 1 cube) (35 cals)

200g (7oz) cauliflower, cut into small florets (68 cals)

200g (7oz) green beans, fresh or frozen, trimmed (48 cals)

1 handful of fresh coriander (10g), chopped (optional) (3 cals)

- Wash the lemon in hot soapy water and dry. Cut in half lengthways and then cut into very thin slices.
- Using a large lidded frying pan (skillet) or casserole dish, heat the oil over a medium–high heat. When hot, add the chicken and red onion and brown the chicken on all sides.
- Stir in the curry powder, turmeric and rice, then pour in the hot stock.
- Add the cauliflower, beans and sliced lemon to the pan. Bring to the boil, reduce the heat and simmer with the lid on for 10 minutes. The chicken should be cooked through and the rice tender. Stir in the coriander and serve.

CHICKEN WITH GINGER AND MANGO SAUCE

234 calories

Chicken and mango go so well together, and combined with fresh herbs and ginger, this dish will become a firm favourite. Serve with rice and green vegetables.

Serves 2 • Ready in 25 minutes

2 × 150g (5oz) skinless, boneless chicken breasts, cut in half lengthways (318 cals)

½ tsp chopped fresh rosemary

½ tsp chopped fresh thyme

salt and freshly ground black pepper

1 tsp olive oil (27 cals)

100g (3½oz) mango pieces, chopped into

small pieces (65 cals)

2 tsp brown sugar (36 cals)

1 tbsp red wine vinegar (2 cals)

1 tbsp dry sherry (14 cals)

1 small thumb fresh root ginger, peeled and finely grated (5 cals)

- Rub the chicken breast pieces with the herbs and a little salt and pepper.
- Heat the olive oil in a large frying pan (skillet) over a medium heat. Add the chicken and fry until golden brown and cooked through, about 8–10 minutes on each side. Remove the chicken from the pan with a slotted spoon, cover and keep warm.
- Return the pan to a medium heat, add the mango and fry for 2 minutes, then add the sugar, vinegar, sherry and ginger, stir well and continue to fry for a further 2 minutes. Pour the mango sauce over the chicken to serve.

MIDDLE EASTERN CHICKEN

272 calories

The chicken needs to be marinated for eight hours or overnight, but then it's quick to cook and serve.

Serves 2 • Ready in 15 minutes (+overnight marinade)

2 × 150g (5oz) skinless, boneless chicken breasts, thinly sliced (318 cals)

1 tsp olive oil (27 cals)

For the marinade:

2 level tbsp low-fat natural yogurt (17 cals)

1 garlic clove, peeled and crushed (3 cals)

salt and freshly ground black pepper

1 cardamom pod

½ tsp allspice

juice of ½ lemon (2 cals)

For the sauce:

1 level tsp tahini (sesame seed paste) (91 cals)

½ garlic clove, peeled and crushed (2 cals)

juice of 1 lemon (2 cals)

1 level tbsp low-fat natural yogurt (8 cals)

For the salad:

½ iceberg lettuce (200g/7oz), shredded (26 cals)

2 spring onions (scallions), trimmed and shredded (9 cals)

2 medium tomatoes, thinly sliced (29 cals)

100g (3½oz) cucumber, peeled and thinly sliced (10 cals)

- Mix all the marinade ingredients together in a large shallow bowl and add the chicken strips. Turn the chicken until it is well coated in the marinade, then cover and chill in the refrigerator for 8 hours, or overnight.

- When you are ready to cook the chicken, make the sauce by simply combining all the sauce ingredients in a small bowl and stirring well.
- Heat the oil in a wok or wide frying pan (skillet) over a mediumhigh heat. When it's sizzling hot, toss in the chicken, including any marinade, and stir-fry for 6–8 minutes or until cooked through.
- Pile the salad ingredients onto 2 serving plates and arrange the chicken on top. Serve the sauce separately or drizzled over.

POSH CHICKEN KIEV

224 calories

These chicken breasts are stuffed with garlicky cream cheese and wrapped in prosciutto. Serve on a bed of salad leaves.

Serves 2 • Ready in 35 minutes

½ tsp olive oil (14 cals)

1 garlic clove, peeled and very finely chopped (3 cals)

2 tbsp extra-light cream cheese (59 cals)

2 × 150g (5oz) skinless, boneless chicken breasts (318 cals)

2 slices Parma ham (prosciutto) (54 cals)

- Preheat the oven to 200C/fan 180C/400F.
- Heat the olive oil in a small frying pan (skillet) and gently fry the garlic for 1–2 minutes until starting to brown. Remove from the heat and stir in the cream cheese.
- Prepare the chicken by making a slit down one side of the chicken breast to make a pocket, then fill each pocket equally with the garlicky cream cheese mixture. (This can get messy!) Wrap each chicken breast with a slice of Parma ham (prosciutto) and put onto a baking sheet (cookie sheet). Cook in the oven for 20–25 minutes or until the chicken is thoroughly cooked. Serve immediately.

CHICKEN SALAD WITH LEMON PEPPER DRESSING

294 calories

This salad is so easy to put together for a quick lunch or light dinner.

Serves 1 • Ready in 5 minutes

1 tbsp low-fat crème fraîche (57 cals)

juice of ½ lemon (2 cals)

freshly ground black pepper

pinch of salt

pinch of sugar (4 cals)

1 × 80g (3oz) bag baby leaf or herb salad (16 cals)

5cm (2in) piece cucumber, finely sliced (10 cals)

1 medium tomato, sliced (14 cals)

1 cooked chicken breast (125g/4oz) (191 cals)

- Combine the crème fraîche, lemon juice, black pepper, salt and sugar in a small bowl.
- Arrange the salad leaves, cucumber and tomato in a wide bowl.
- Cut the chicken into thick slices and arrange on top of the salad. Drizzle the dressing over and serve.

SWEET ONION CHICKEN

235 calories

This is a hot and spicy yet fresh chicken dish. If you don't like too much spice, then deseed the chillies before using. Remember not to rub your face and eyes when handling chillies and to wash your hands, the knife and chopping (cutting) board after chopping them.

Serves 2 • Ready in 30 minutes

2 tsp sunflower oil (54 cals)

1 medium onion, peeled and finely chopped (65 cals)

2 bird's eye (Thai) chillies, finely chopped (1 cal)

3 garlic cloves, peeled and grated (9 cals)

2.5cm (1in) piece fresh root ginger, peeled and grated (5 cals)

a pinch of salt

1 tomato, diced (14 cals)

2 × 150g (5oz) skinless, boneless chicken breasts, cut into cubes (318 cals)

½ tsp ground cumin

1 tsp coarsely ground black pepper

1 small handful of fresh coriander (cilantro), chopped (3 cals)

- Heat the oil in a wide frying pan (skillet) over a medium-high heat. When hot, add the onion, chillies, garlic, ginger and salt and stir-fry for 2 minutes before reducing the heat and cooking gently for a further 5 minutes.
- Increase the heat to medium, toss in the tomato and stir-fry for 2 minutes. Add the chicken, cumin and pepper and stir-fry for a further 5 minutes.
- Reduce the heat to low, pour in 150ml (generous ½ cup) water, stir and cook for another 5 minutes. If there seems to be too much liquid, increase the heat and boil for 1–2 minutes. Stir in the coriander (cilantro) before serving.

HARISSA ROASTED CHICKEN, SHALLOTS AND SWEET POTATO

261 calories

This is a great combination of flavours and is very simple to put together.

Serves 1 • Ready in 30 minutes plus 30 minutes marinating

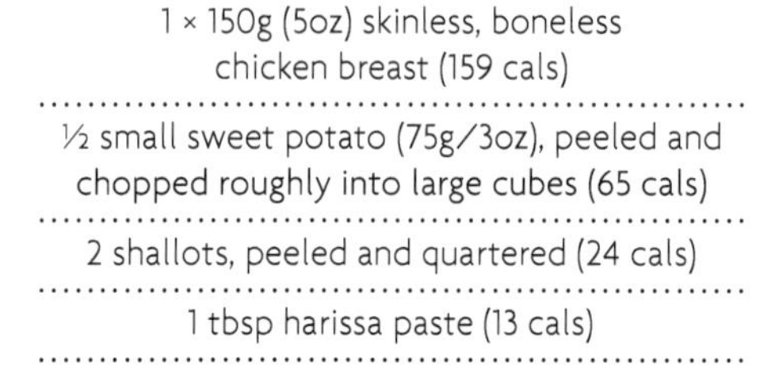

1 × 150g (5oz) skinless, boneless chicken breast (159 cals)

½ small sweet potato (75g/3oz), peeled and chopped roughly into large cubes (65 cals)

2 shallots, peeled and quartered (24 cals)

1 tbsp harissa paste (13 cals)

- Cut the chicken breast into 3 or 4 pieces and place in a bowl with the sweet potato and shallots.
- In a small bowl, combine the harissa paste with 1 tablespoon water. Pour over the chicken and vegetables and mix thoroughly, making sure everything is coated. Cover and leave to marinate for about 30 minutes.
- Preheat the oven to 220C/fan 200C/425F.
- Transfer the chicken and vegetables to a wide baking dish and cook in the oven for 18–25 minutes. Check that the chicken is cooked through before serving.

CAJUN FRIED CHICKEN

193 calories (including 9 cals from spice mix)

The spice mix here is enough to make 6–8 portions, so make a batch and store the rest of the spices in an airtight container or jar.

Serves 1 • Ready in 15 minutes

1 × 150g (5oz) skinless chicken breast (159 cals)

1 tsp sunflower oil (27 cals)

For the spice mix (69 cals in total):

5 tsp ground cumin

2 heaped tsp smoked paprika (28 cals)

2 heaped tsp hot paprika (28 cals)

2 tsp dried thyme (3 cals)

2 tsp dried oregano (6 cals)

½ tsp cayenne pepper (2 cals)

1 tsp salt

- For the spice mix, mix together the spices and salt.
- Cut the chicken into 4–5 strips. Sprinkle 2 teaspoons of the spice mix over and use your hands to toss.
- Heat the oil in a shallow frying pan (skillet) over a medium-high heat. When hot, toss in the chicken and cook for 4-5 minutes on each side, until golden and cooked through. Serve.

FRAGRANT CHICKEN

333 calories

Serves 2 • Ready in 30 minutes

1 tsp olive oil (27 cals)

1 small onion, peeled and finely chopped (22 cals)

½ tsp cumin seeds

½ tsp turmeric

300ml (1¼ cups) fresh chicken stock (21 cals)

½ lemon (2 cals)

2 × 150g (5oz) skinless chicken breasts, diced (318 cals)

200g (7oz) new potatoes, quartered (140 cals)

few strands of saffron

10g (2 tsp) butter (74 cals)

12 large black olives, pitted (62 cals)

4 fresh basil leaves, roughly chopped

salt and freshly ground black pepper

- Heat the oil in a pan over a low heat, add the onion and sweat for 7–8 minutes. Add the cumin seeds and turmeric and fry for 1–2 minutes until aromatic.
- Pour in the chicken stock and bring to a gentle simmer. Add the lemon zest then cut out the flesh of the lemon, roughly chop and add to the pan.
- Add the chicken, potatoes and saffron. Bring back to simmering point and cook gently for 10 minutes until the potatoes are tender and the chicken is cooked through. Remove the chicken and potatoes from the pan and keep warm.
- Increase the heat under the pan to high and stir in the butter, olives, basil and salt and pepper. Bubble over a high heat for 2–4 minutes until the sauce is a little thicker and glossy. Pour the sauce over the chicken and potatoes and serve immediately.

OLIVE CHICKEN AND BROCCOLI

250 calories

Serves 2 • Ready in 20 minutes

2 × 150g (5oz) skinless chicken breasts (318 cals)

2 shallots (12 cals)

1 bay leaf

200g (7oz) head broccoli, cut into florets (66 cals)

1 tsp olive oil (27 cals)

1 garlic clove, peeled and finely sliced (3 cals)

1 small red chilli, deseeded and finely chopped (4 cals)

12 large black olives, pitted (62 cals)

2 tbsp light soy sauce (9 cals)

- Place the chicken breasts in the base of a lidded saucepan, together with 1 of the shallots cut in half and the bay leaf. Pour on boiling water until generously covered and bring to a gentle simmer for 5 minutes. Turn off the heat, put the lid on and leave the chicken to cook for a further 5 minutes. Check the chicken is cooked through before removing from the pan. Leave to cool slightly before cutting into slices.
- Boil the broccoli by submerging in boiling water and simmering for 6 minutes until tender. Drain and set aside.
- Chop the remaining shallot into fine half rings. Heat the olive oil in a wide frying pan (skillet) over a medium heat and lightly fry the shallot until golden and soft. Add the garlic and chilli and fry for a further 2 minutes.
- Stir in the cooked chicken and broccoli, together with the olives. Finally, add the soy sauce and warm through before serving.

CHICKEN FOO YOUNG

325 calories

This classic Chinese-Indonesian egg dish can be prepared, cooked and on your plate in less than 10 minutes.

Serves 2 • Ready in 10 minutes

2 tsp olive oil (54 cals)

3 large free-range eggs, beaten (297 cals)

3 spring onions (scallions), trimmed and shredded (14 cals)

½ garlic clove, peeled and finely chopped (2 cals)

250g cooked chicken, cut into small pieces (265 cals)

1 tbsp dry sherry (14 cals)

1 small handful of fresh coriander (cilantro) leaves, chopped (3 cals)

salt and freshly ground black pepper

- Heat 1 teaspoon of olive oil in a wide saucepan or wok, add the eggs and scramble lightly, removing them from the pan while they are still a little runny and just before they are fully cooked. Transfer to a bowl, cover and set aside.
- Heat the remaining oil, add the spring onions (scallions) and garlic and gently fry for a minute, then add the chicken and fry for a further 2 minutes. Add the sherry and coriander (cilantro), season to taste with salt and pepper and stir in the reserved eggs. Cook for a further minute before serving.

PARMESAN CHICKEN

266 calories

Serves 2 • Ready in 15 minutes

20g (4 tsp) Parmesan, finely grated (90 cals)

1 tsp plain (all-purpose) flour (17 cals)

salt and freshly ground black pepper

1 egg white (9 cals)

2 × 150g (5oz) skinless chicken breast, halved (318 cals)

70g (2½ oz) peas, fresh or frozen (58 cals)

50g (1¾oz) baby spinach leaves (12 cals)

1 tsp extra virgin olive oil (27 cals)

1 tsp white wine vinegar (1 cal)

- Preheat the grill to a medium setting. Loosely mix the Parmesan, flour and a little salt and pepper on a plate. Beat the egg white in a wide bowl.
- Dip each piece of chicken first in the egg white and then in the Parmesan, making sure it is lightly coated on both sides.
- Place the chicken pieces on a grill tray and cook under the grill for 5–6 minutes on each side until golden and cooked through. While the chicken is cooking, cook the peas in boiling water for 6 minutes until tender.
- Drain the peas and return to the pan. Stir through the spinach, allowing it to wilt slightly in the heat. Add the olive oil and vinegar and stir through.
- Transfer to 2 serving plates and arrange 2 pieces of chicken each on top of the green vegetables.

CHICKEN, RICE AND PEAS

424 calories

This warming dish for one is a saviour on a cold winter's night. It's easy to cook and is so so satisfying.

Serves 1 • Ready in 30 minutes

30g basmati rice (dry weight) (108 cals)

50g (scant ½ cup) frozen peas (33 cals)

1 tsp olive oil (27 cals)

1 × 150g (5oz) skinless chicken breast, cut into strips (159 cals)

75ml skimmed milk (28 cals)

½ tbsp light soft cheese (27 cals)

10g (2 tbsp) mature (sharp) Cheddar, grated (41 cals)

salt and freshly ground black pepper

- Boil the rice as per the packet instructions. Add the frozen peas 6 minutes before the end of the cooking time. Drain and set aside.
- Heat the olive oil in a frying pan (skillet) over a medium heat and fry the chicken for 6-8 minutes, until browned all over.
- Add the milk, soft cheese and Cheddar to the frying pan. Bring to a gentle simmer and continue to cook gently for 5 minutes.
- Finally, add the cooked rice and peas to the pan and heat through. Season with salt and pepper.
- Serve immediately.

Healthy Diet Recipes

SOUPS & STEWS

Fresh, Healthy and Easy Recipes
from best-selling cookery author,
Jacqueline Whitehart.

Healthy Diet Recipes: Soups & Stews

HEARTY ROOT VEGETABLE SOUP

CARROT AND CORIANDER SOUP

RAINY DAY STEW

HOT AND SOUR NOODLE SOUP

SLOW-BAKED CHICKEN ROLLS IN TOMATO SAUCE

MISO BROTH

CARIBBEAN CASSEROLE

FRESH TOMATO AND CHILLI SOUP

QUICK ITALIAN BEEF STEW

LAMB TAGINE

CHUNKY VEGETABLE SOUP

APPLE AND CELERIAC SOUP

BORSCHT (CHUNKY BEETROOT SOUP)

LAMB POT ROAST

ASIAN CHICKEN BROTH

CHORIZO AND TOMATO SOUP

TRADITIONAL GOULASH

PEAR AND PARSNIP SOUP

CREAMY PEA AND MINT SOUP

BEEF BOURGUIGNON

LENTIL, LEMON AND THYME SOUP

SAVOY CABBAGE AND STILTON SOUP

SLOW ONION SOUP

MUSHROOM AND BACON SOUP

SPRING CHICKEN STEW

RED PEPPER AND GOAT'S CHEESE SOUP

HAM, LENTIL AND PEARL BARLEY SOUP

Healthy Diet Recipes: Soups & Stews

This new set of easy diet recipes are designed to be easy to follow, quick recipes that you can with little fuss. I love cooking for myself and my family but often find that cookbooks tend towards the 'special' or 'weekend' recipes whereas what we want 99% of the time is something simple and healthy that we can make from scratch and avoid the dreaded processed or ready meals. All the recipes are carefully crafted to be well-balanced and healthy and are calorie-counted for your convenience. Most if not all recipes can be kept or frozen in individual portions to provide several days worth of healthy meals.

The Soups and Stews Collection includes old favourites as well as some seasonal and unusual flavours to keep it interesting. A soup or stew is such a filling and healthy alternative to a sandwich or pasta and are always simple to make. Replacing a sandwich with soup and a pasta dinner with a flavoursome stew is probably one of the simplest and effective way to lose weight.

HEARTY ROOT VEGETABLE SOUP

100 calories

You can't get anything more warming and filling for 100 calories.

Serves 4 • Ready in 35 minutes

1 potato (170g/6oz) (128 cals)

2 medium carrots (70 cals)

1 small swede, about 300g/11oz (72 cals)

1 turnip (80g/3oz) (18 cals)

1 medium parsnip (80g/3oz) (51 cals)

1 leek, trimmed and sliced (26 cals)

1 litre vegetable stock (fresh or made with 1 cube) (35 cals)

salt and freshly ground black pepper

- Peel and roughly chop the root vegetables.
- Place all the vegetables and the stock in a large saucepan and bring to the boil. Put the lid on, reduce the heat and simmer gently for 20 minutes.
- Blend in a blender or food processor until smooth, then return the soup to the pan and reheat gently, adding a little water if it is too thick.
- Season generously to taste and serve.

CARROT AND CORIANDER SOUP

116 calories

This classic soup is a breeze to make.

Serves 4 • Ready in 35 minutes

1 large onion, peeled and chopped (86 cals)

500g (1lb 2oz) carrots, about 6 medium (175 cals)

1 small potato (100g/3oz), peeled and chopped (75 cals)

1 tsp ground coriander

1 litre (4 cups) vegetable stock (fresh or made with 2 cubes) (70 cals)

large handful of fresh coriander

To serve

freshly ground black pepper

2 tsp extra virgin olive oil (54 cals)

- Simply place the onion, carrots, potato and ground coriander in a large saucepan and pour in the stock. Bring to the boil, reduce the heat and simmer for 20 minutes until tender.
- Blitz in a blender or food processor with the fresh coriander until smooth. Return the soup to the pan and reheat gently.
- Serve with lashings of black pepper, salt to taste and a drizzle (½ teaspoon) of extra virgin olive oil.

RAINY DAY STEW

312 calories

As its name suggests this recipe is a light and easy stew for a wet evening.

Serves 2 • Ready in 45 minutes

1 litre (4 cups) chicken stock (fresh is best here) (70 cals)

1 leek, trimmed and sliced (26 cals)

2 Cumberland sausages, sliced into 2cm pieces (207 cals)

1 red chilli, deseeded if preferred and sliced (4 cals) 1 Parmesan rind (for flavour only, removed after cooking)

2 bay leaves

½ tsp dried mixed herbs or small handful of fresh basil and/or parsley if available

1 courgette (zucchini), halved and sliced (27 cals)

50g peas, fresh or frozen (42 cals)

50g (1¾oz) macaroni (or other small pasta) (174 cals)

2 medium tomatoes, diced (29 cals) salt and freshly ground black pepper

10g fresh Parmesan, grated (45 cals)

- Heat the chicken stock in a large saucepan with the leek, sausages, chilli, Parmesan rind, bay leaves and dried herbs. Bring to a gentle simmer and cook for about 25 minutes.
- Add the courgette (zucchini), peas and macaroni and simmer for a further 10–15 minutes until the pasta and peas are tender.
- Remove the Parmesan rind and bay leaves from the pan and add the tomatoes and any fresh herbs if using.
- Serve in large bowls and season generously. Sprinkle the grated Parmesan over the top.

HOT AND SOUR NOODLE SOUP

115 calories

This Wagamama's inspired soup is comforting and revitalising in equal measure. I use the amazing konjac noodles (made from a zero calorie Japanese root) to make this soup so low calorie. Konjac noodles, also called Shiritaki noodles, can be bought from a Chinese supermarket or online.

Serves 1 • Ready in 15 minutes

250ml (1 cup) chicken stock (18 cals)

250ml (1 cup) water

1 tbsp (25g/1oz) miso paste (41 cals)

3 spring onions (scallions), peeled and shredded (15 cals)

½ carrot, peeled and cut into matchsticks (17 cals)

½ stick lemongrass, finely shredded

Small thumb ginger, peeled and cut into matchsticks (9 cals)

1 red chilli, de-seeded and cut into rings (2 cals)

100g (3½oz) mushrooms, washed and sliced (13 cals)

200g (7oz) konjac noodles

1 tsp rice vinegar

- Bring the chicken stock, water and miso paste to a gentle simmer. Add the spring onions, carrot, lemongrass, ginger, chilli and mushrooms. Cook gently for 10 minutes.
- Drain the noodles through a sieve and rinse under the tap for about a minute. Place the noodles in a wide frying pan and heat on a high heat for 5-7 minutes, stirring occasionally, until the noodles are dry and no longer steaming.
- Transfer the noodles to a wide bowl. Add the rice vinegar to the hot soup and pour over the noodles. Serve immediately.

SLOW-BAKED CHICKEN ROLLS IN TOMATO SAUCE

274 calories

This is a great one-pot dish where you just pop your ingredients in the casserole dish and leave it to cook slowly.

Serves 4 • Ready in 3 hours

100g (3½oz) sausagemeat (309 cals)

4 skinless, boneless chicken thighs, about 370g/13oz (392 cals)

1 onion, peeled and chopped (654 cals)

2 garlic cloves, peeled and finely chopped (6 cals)

1 red (bell) pepper, deseeded and roughly chopped (45 cals)

1 green (bell) pepper, deseeded and roughly chopped (24 cals)

1 × 400g (14oz) can butter (lima) beans, rinsed and drained (182 cals)

1 × 400g (14oz) can chopped tomatoes (64 cals)

½ chicken stock (bouillon) cube (18 cals)

1 tsp dried oregano (3 cals)

- Preheat the oven to 140C/120C fan/275F if using the oven.
- Divide the sausagemeat into roughly 4 equal portions. Open up the chicken thighs and lay them flat. Place the portion of sausagemeat in the middle of the chicken and pull up the sides so that the meat is enclosed in a tight roll. If you wish to make a neater parcel you can hold the two ends of the chicken together with a cocktail stick (toothpick). Turn the chicken roll over so that the join is on the bottom.
- Use a large casserole dish or slow cooker dish. Layer the onion, garlic and peppers at the base of the dish, then add the butter

(lima) beans. Place the stuffed chicken thighs on top and pour on the chopped tomatoes. Crunch up the stock (bouillon) cube in your fingers and sprinkle over the top. Add the oregano. Finally, top up with 300ml (1¼ cups) water until the chicken is generously covered.

- Cook in the oven for 3 hours. Alternatively, cook in the slow cooker for at least 6 hours.

MISO BROTH

117 calories

This soup is filling, satisfying and easy to make in about 10 minutes.

Serves 1 • Ready in 10 minutes

1 heaped tbsp miso soup paste (35 cals)

1 tsp mirin (rice wine) (14 cals)

1 tbsp dark soy sauce, plus extra for drizzling (4 cals)

1 tsp nam pla (Thai fish sauce) (4 cals)

1cm (½in) piece fresh root ginger, peeled and grated (5 cals)

50g (1¾oz) spring greens or Savoy cabbage, thinly sliced (14 cals)

½ carrot, peeled and cut into very fine batons (13 cals)

50g (1¾oz) beansprouts (16 cals)

50g (1¾oz) shiitake mushrooms, sliced (12 cals)

- Bring 500ml water to boiling point in a large saucepan. Stir in the miso soup paste, mirin, soy, nam pla and ginger, then add the greens, carrot, beansprouts & mushrooms and simmer gently for 5m. Serve in a wide bowl with soy sauce drizzled over the top.

CARIBBEAN CASSEROLE

251 calories

A flavoursome vegetarian casserole, this couldn't be simpler – you just throw it all in!

Serves 4 • Ready in 3 hours

1 large onion, peeled and chopped (86 cals)

1 red (bell) pepper, chopped (51 cals)

2 green chillies, deseeded and chopped (6 cals)

2 medium sweet potatoes, peeled and cut into wedges (150g/5oz) (261 cals)

1 × 400g (14oz) can chopped tomatoes (64 cals)

2 tbsp shop-bought salsa (12 cals)

1 × 200g (7oz) can pineapple chunks in juice, drained (137 cals)

1 cooking apple, peeled, cored and roughly chopped (35 cals)

250ml (generous 1 cup) vegetable stock (made with ½ cube) (18 cals)

1 × 400g (14oz) can butter (lima) beans, rinsed and drained (220 cals)

1 tbsp dark brown sugar (54 cals)

1 tbsp desiccated (dry unsweetened) coconut (60 cals)

1 tsp chilli powder

½ tsp ground cumin

½ tsp dried oregano (2 cals)

pinch of ground cinnamon

- Preheat the oven to 160C/140C fan/325F.
- Place all the ingredients in a large casserole dish, put on the lid and cook in the oven for 2½ hours. Check the water levels halfway through cooking.
- Alternatively, cook in a slow cooker for about 6 hours.

FRESH TOMATO AND CHILLI SOUP

123 calories

This soup is best made when the tomatoes are cheap and flavoursome. I go for the easy option – no peeling or deseeding tomatoes here!

Serves 4 • Ready in 35 minutes

1 tbsp olive oil (99 cals)

2 medium onions, peeled and cut into thin half rings (108 cals)

2 red chillies, deseeded and diced (4 cals)

1 red pepper, deseeded and chopped (51 cals)

salt and freshly ground black pepper

2 tbsp tomato puree (60 cals)

1kg (2lb 2oz) ripe tomatoes, very roughly chopped (170 cals)

- Heat the oil in a large lidded frying pan over a medium heat. Add the onions, chillies and red (bell) pepper and fry for 3 minutes. Season generously with salt and pepper, then reduce the heat, put the lid on and cook slowly for 20 minutes, until tender.
- Increase the heat back and stir in the tomato puree. Cook for 1 minute, then add the tomatoes, stir and put the lid back on. Reduce the heat to low and cook for a further 10 minutes.
- Stir and break up the some of the tomatoes with the back of the spoon. Remove any loose tomato skins – you don't need to be perfectionist about this, I normally remove about half. If the soup is too thick add a little water and bring it back up to temperature. Adjust the seasoning if necessary and then serve.

QUICK ITALIAN BEEF STEW

229 calories

Serves 2 • Ready in 40 minutes

1 tsp sunflower oil (27 cals)

200g (7oz) lean beef strips (246 cals)

salt and freshly ground black pepper

½ onion, peeled and sliced into half rings (27 cals)

1 garlic clove, peeled and thinly sliced (3 cals)

½ green (bell) pepper, deseeded and sliced (10 cals)

½ yellow (bell) pepper, deseeded and sliced (18 cals)

1 × 400g (14oz) can chopped tomatoes (64 cals)

½ tsp dried mixed herbs

a little fresh oregano (optional)

12 large black olives, pitted (62 cals)

- Heat the oil in a large pan over a high heat. Season the beef with salt and pepper. When the oil is hot, toss in the beef and stir-fry for 2 minutes. Remove the beef from the pan and set aside.
- Reduce the heat to medium and fry the onion, garlic and (bell) peppers for 5–10 minutes until tender. With the heat still at medium, add the tomatoes and herbs and simmer for 15 minutes.
- Stir through the beef strips and olives and heat for a further 2 minutes before serving.

LAMB TAGINE

303 calories

This delicious concoction is sweet and spicy. I have adapted the traditional recipe here to suit my own needs – it really works. Most of the ingredients are storecupboard favourites, so it is a breeze to put together.

Serves 4 • Ready in 2 hours

1 tbsp vegetable oil (99 cals)

1 tbsp plain (all-purpose) flour, seasoned with salt and freshly ground black pepper (68 cals)

300g (11oz) extra lean diced lamb (459 cals)

1 medium onion, chopped (54 cals)

2 tsp mild chilli powder

1 tsp turmeric

1 tsp ground cumin

1 × 400g (14oz) can chopped tomatoes (64 cals)

500ml (generous 2 cups) lamb/chicken or vegetable stock (made with 1 cube) (35 cals)

100g (½ cup) pearl barley (360 cals)

1 tbsp shop-bought salsa (7 cals)

1 tbsp apricot jam (63 cals)

juice of 1 lime (4 cals)

- Preheat the oven to 180C/160C fan/350F if using. Heat the oil in a large lidded casserole dish over a high heat.
- Sprinkle the seasoned flour over the diced lamb and use your hands to mix it through and make sure all the surfaces of the meat are covered.
- When the oil is hot, toss in the meat and fry for about 2 minutes without stirring. Then stir, turn and fry the other side for a further 2 minutes. Remove the lamb from the dish with a slotted spoon.

- Turn the heat down to low and add the onion. Stir in the spices, then add the chopped tomatoes and stock. Bring to the boil. Add the pearl barley and boil vigorously for 10 minutes.
- Return the lamb to the casserole. Stir in the salsa, jam and lime juice. Put the lid on and cook in the oven for 2 hours OR transfer to a slow cooker and cook on low for 6–8 hours.

CHUNKY VEGETABLE SOUP

128 calories

This is a really simple and tasty vegetable soup. It has loads of different vegetables in it. If you don't have them all, just leave one or two out and adjust the calories accordingly.

You make an enormous batch and keep/freeze in individual portions.

Serves 6 • Ready in 1hr 10mins

1 tsp olive oil (27 cals)

1 large onion, peeled and chopped (72 cals)

2 garlic cloves, peeled and finely sliced (6 cals)

2 leeks, trimmed & cut fine rings (52 cals)

2 carrots, peeled and chopped into large chunks (58 cals)

1 small swede, peeled and chopped into large chunks (44 cals)

1 sweet potato, peeled and chopped into large chunks (124 cals)

1 × 400g (14oz) can chopped tomatoes (64 cals)

1 tbsp tomato purée (30 cals)

2 bay leaves

1 handful of fresh coriander (cilantro) stalks, roughly chopped (optional)

1 chicken / vegetable stock cube (35 cals)

80g (3oz) frozen peas (53 cals)

1 x 400g (14oz) can cannellini beans, drained and rinsed (210 cals)

salt and freshly ground black pepper

- Heat the olive oil in a medium-sized lidded saucepan, add the onion and garlic and fry very gently for 5 minutes. Add the leek, carrots, swede and sweet potato and stir well.

- Add the canned tomatoes, tomato purée, bay leaves and coriander stalks to the pan, then crumble in the stock cube. Top up with about 1 litre water. Bring the mixture to the boil, cover with a lid, then reduce the heat and simmer very gently on the lowest heat for 45 minutes. Add the peas and cannellini beans and simmer for a further 5 minutes or until the peas are cooked. Season with salt and pepper to taste and serve.

APPLE AND CELERIAC SOUP

62 calories

Easy, tasty and exceptionally low in calories.

Serves 4 • Ready in 35 mins

- 1 onion, peeled and chopped (54 cals)
- 1 large cooking apple, peeled and chopped (54 cals)
- ½ medium celeriac, about 350g (12oz), peeled and chopped (63 cals)
- 1 litre vegetable stock (fresh or made with 2 cubes) (70 cals)
- 1 tsp curry powder (7 cals)
- 1 tsp mixed dried herbs
- Salt and freshly ground black pepper

- Put the onion, apple and celeriac in a large saucepan and pour over the stock. Bring to the boil. Add the curry powder and mixed herbs then reduce the heat and simmer for 20–25 minutes until tender.
- Blend until smooth, then return the soup to the pan and bring back to temperature before serving. If the soup is a little thick, stir in some water until the desired consistency is achieved. Season with salt and pepper before serving.

BORSCHT (CHUNKY BEETROOT SOUP)

134 calories

This is a Russian soup and I have left it chunky in the Russian style, but you could purée it if you prefer. I use a vacuum pack of cooked beetroot for simplicity, making sure they are in natural juices not vinegar.

Serves 4 • Ready in 35 minutes

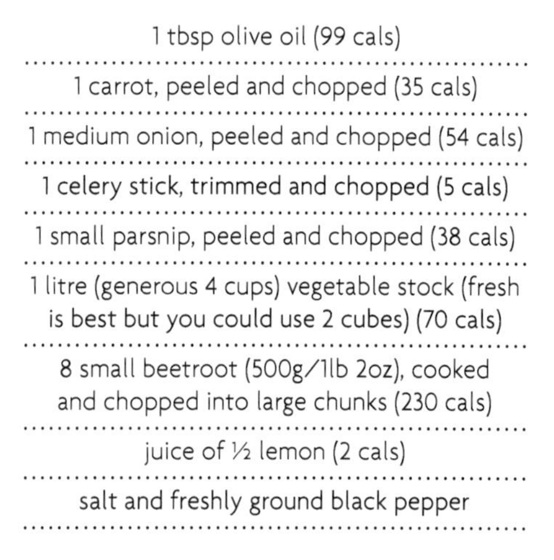

1 tbsp olive oil (99 cals)

1 carrot, peeled and chopped (35 cals)

1 medium onion, peeled and chopped (54 cals)

1 celery stick, trimmed and chopped (5 cals)

1 small parsnip, peeled and chopped (38 cals)

1 litre (generous 4 cups) vegetable stock (fresh is best but you could use 2 cubes) (70 cals)

8 small beetroot (500g/1lb 2oz), cooked and chopped into large chunks (230 cals)

juice of ½ lemon (2 cals)

salt and freshly ground black pepper

- Heat the oil in a large lidded saucepan over a low heat, add the carrot, onion, celery and parsnip, then stir and put the lid on. Allow the vegetables to sweat for 10 minutes.
- Add the stock, bring to the boil, then reduce the heat and simmer with the lid off for 10 minutes. Add the beetroot and simmer for another 5 minutes.
- Add the lemon juice and pepper to taste.

LAMB POT ROAST

367 calories

A warming and easy dish.

Serves 4 • Ready in 3 hours

4 × 90g (3¼oz) lean lamb leg steaks (673 cals)

2 tsp turmeric

2 tsp English mustard (22 cals)

1 tsp sugar (16 cals)

salt and freshly ground black pepper

1 tbsp vegetable oil (99 cals)

1 medium onion, peeled and chopped (54 cals)

4 garlic cloves, peeled and chopped (12 cals)

1 medium sweet potato (about 130g/4½oz), peeled and cut into large chunks (113 cals)

1 × 400g (14oz) can whole tomatoes (64 cals)

1 × 400g (14oz) can chickpeas, rinsed and drained (276 cals)

500ml (generous 2 cups) lamb or chicken stock (made from 1 stock cube) (35 cals)

100g (3½oz) spinach, fresh or frozen (about 4 cubes) (21 cals)

100g (scant 1 cup) peas, fresh (83 cals)

- Rub the lamb all over with the turmeric, mustard, sugar and salt and pepper.
- In a casserole dish, heat the vegetable oil until it is smoking hot. Toss in the lamb and fry for 2 minutes each side. Reduce the heat and stir in the onion and garlic and fry gently for 2 minutes.
- Add the sweet potato, tomatoes, chickpeas and stock, then stir and put the lid on.
- In the oven: Preheat the oven to 180C/160C fan/350F and cook for

2 hours.

- Stir in the spinach and peas. Replace onto the hob, bring to a gentle simmer and cook for 10 minutes.
- In the slow cooker: Cook on low for 7–8 hours. Stir in the spinach and peas. Turn to high and cook uncovered for 30 minutes.

ASIAN CHICKEN BROTH

135 calories

This soup somehow manages to be both fresh and warming at the same time. Great for when you have the sniffles too. Warning! It's quite hot and spicy, so feel free to cut down the chilli if necessary.

Serves 4 • Ready in 30 mins

1 litre (generous 4 cups) fresh chicken stock (70 cals)

2 chillis, de-seeded and chopped into rings (4 cals)

6 spring onions (scallions), shredded (30 cals)

1 thumb ginger, peeled and cut into very thin strips (10 cals)

Zest of 1 lime

pinch of mace

1 red (bell) pepper, de-seeded and cut into strips (51 cals)

1 tsp rice vinegar (1 cal)

1 tsp nam pla (fish sauce) (4 cals)

200g (7oz) fine beans, trimmed (70 cals)

1x400g (14oz) can low fat coconut milk (292)

Juice of 2 limes (8 cals)

Salt and pepper to taste

- Heat the chicken stock with the chillis, spring onions, ginger, lime zest, mace and red pepper. Add a pinch of mace, nam pla and rice vinegar and simmer for 20m.
- Stir in the fine beans and coconut milk. Bring up to a gentle simmer and cook until the beans are just tender. Add the lime juice and season before serving.

CHORIZO AND TOMATO SOUP

137 cals

This soup feels a little bit naughty because of the chorizo but we only use a little and it adds real depth of flavour to the soup.

Makes 6 servings • Ready in 45 mins

1 tsp olive oil (27 cals)

1 onion, diced (65 cals)

1 garlic clove, finely sliced (4 cals)

1 green pepper, diced (24 cals)

80g chorizo, diced (232 cals)

1 litre vegetable stock, fresh or made with one stock cube (35 cals)

1x400g (14oz) can chopped tomatoes (64 cals)

300g passata (strained tomatoes) (93 cals)

1x400g (14oz) can chickpeas, rinsed and drained (276 cals)

- Heat the oil in a saucepan, add the onion and cook gently for 5 minutes. Add the garlic, green pepper and chorizo, then cook for a further 5 minutes. Add the stock, tomatoes, passata and chickpeas, then simmer for 30 minutes.

TRADITIONAL GOULASH

324 calories

This delicious Hungarian dish is a favourite in our household.

Serves 4 • Ready in 2½ hours

400g (14oz) extra lean casserole beef steak, diced (492 cals)

1 tbsp plain (all-purpose) flour (68 cals)

salt and freshly ground black pepper

2 tbsp sunflower oil (198 cals)

1 large onion, chopped (86 cals)

2 garlic cloves, peeled and chopped (6 cals)

1 green (bell) pepper, deseeded and chopped (21 cals)

1 red (bell) pepper, deseeded and chopped (45 cals)

1 heaped tbsp paprika (42 cals)

1 heaped tsp smoked paprika (14 cals)

1 × 400g (14oz) can chopped tomatoes (64 cals)

250ml (generous 1 cup) beef stock (fresh or made with ½ cube) (18 cals)

150ml (generous ½ cup) light crème fraîche (243 cals)

- Sprinkle the beef with the flour and salt and pepper and toss until well coated.
- Heat the oil in a casserole dish over a high heat. Brown the steak in batches and set aside.
- Turn the heat to low and add the onion, garlic and (bell) peppers. Put the lid on and sweat until tender, about 10 minutes.
- Return the beef to the pan together with both types of paprika, the chopped tomatoes and beef stock. Bring to a simmer and cook with

the lid off for 20–30 minutes.

- On the hob: Continue to cook over a low heat for about 1 hour, removing the lid towards the end of the cooking time.
- In the oven: Preheat the oven to 150C/130C fan/300F and cook for 3 hours.
- In the slow cooker: Transfer to a slow cooker and cook on low for 8 hours or overnight. Stir in the crème fraîche just before serving. The goulash freezes well and this can be done before or after the crème fraîche is added.

PEAR AND PARSNIP SOUP

144 calories

Another classic soup for winter. The pear adds a touch of sweetness. Stock up your freezer, this soup is filling and satisfying.

Serves 4 • Ready in 40 mins

1 tbsp olive oil (99 cals)

1 onion, peeled and chopped (65 cals)

2 tsp medium curry powder (14 cals)

4 parsnips, peeled and roughly chopped (180 cals)

1 stick celery, chopped (5 cals)

2 pears, peeled, cored and chopped (120 cals)

1 litre water

1 vegetable stock cube, crumbled (35 cals)

100g (3½oz) low-fat natural yoghurt (56 cals)

salt and black pepper to taste

- Heat the olive oil gently in a large saucepan or casserole. Fry the onion in the oil for 5 minutes. Stir through the curry powder before adding the parsnips and celery. Place the lid on the pan and sweat the vegetables on a gentle heat for a further 5 minutes.
- Add the chopped pear, water and vegetable stock cube. Bring to the boil and simmer for 20 minutes until the vegetables are tender.
- Pour contents of saucepan into a blender and blend until smooth. Return the soup to the pan. Stir in the yoghurt. Reheat gently and check the seasoning before serving.

CREAMY PEA AND MINT SOUP

151 calories

This unusual soup is has an amazing green colour and tastes so fresh.

Serves 4 • Ready in 20 minutes

1 tbsp olive oil (99 cals)

8 spring onions (scallions), trimmed and roughly chopped (40 cals)

1 iceberg lettuce (400g/14oz), outer leaves removed and roughly chopped (52 cals)

400g (14oz) frozen peas (264 cals)

1 litre vegetable or chicken stock (fresh is best here) (70 cals)

8 fresh mint leaves

100g (3½oz) low-fat Greek yogurt (80 cals)

freshly ground black pepper

- In a large saucepan, heat the oil over a low heat. Stir in the spring onions and lettuce for 1–2 minutes until the lettuce starts to wilt.
- Add the peas, stock and mint leaves. Bring to a gentle simmer and cook for 15 minutes or until all the vegetables are tender.
- Blend the soup until smooth. For an even smoother texture, pass the soup through a sieve after blending.
- Stir in the yogurt and bring back up to temperature before serving. Season with black pepper and serve.

BEEF BOURGUIGNON

359 calories

This is a very simple way to make an unauthentic but still very yummy bourguignon.

Serves 4 • Ready in 3 hours

400g (14oz) extra lean casserole beef steak, diced (492 cals)

100g (3½oz) lardons or bacon bits (276 cals)

200g (7oz) button mushrooms, washed (26 cals)

2 garlic cloves, peeled and sliced (6 cals)

1 medium onion, peeled, halved and sliced (54 cals)

200g (7oz) pickled shallots, drained (30 cals)

1 tsp dried thyme (3 cals)

2 bay leaves

2 tbsp plain (all-purpose) flour (204 cals)

salt and freshly ground black pepper

400ml (1¾ cups) red wine (344 cals)

- Put the beef, lardons, mushrooms, garlic, onion, shallots, thyme and bay leaves into a large casserole dish or slow cooker dish.
- Sprinkle on the flour and, using your hands, toss it around until everything is lightly coated in flour.
- Next, season with salt and pepper and pour on the wine and 100ml (scant ½ cup) water. Give it a stir and pop on the lid.
- In the oven: Preheat the oven to 140C/120C fan/275F and cook for 3 hours.
- In the slow cooker: Cook on low for 8 hours. Add a little water halfway through cooking if necessary.

LENTIL, LEMON AND THYME SOUP

194 calories

This is a great soup that can be made easily from store cupboard ingredients.

Serves 4 • Ready in 50 minutes

1 tbsp olive oil (99 cals)

1 large onion, finely diced (79 cals)

1 garlic clove, finely chopped (4 cals)

150g (5oz) red lentils, rinsed in a sieve (477 cals)

500ml vegetable stock, fresh or made from 1 stock cube (35 cals)

1x400g (14oz) can chopped tomatoes (64 cals)

2 tsp tomato purée (16 cals)

2 tsp dried thyme, or 2 fresh sprigs

juice of ½ lemon (2 cals)

- Heat the oil in a large saucepan and gently fry the onions and garlic for 5 minutes until soft. Add the lentils and stir into the onions. Pour in the stock, then bring to the boil. Simmer vigorously for 10 minutes.
- Reduce the heat and add the thyme, tinned tomatoes and puree. Bring back to a quiet simmer and simmer gently for 30 minutes. Add the lemon juice and season to taste.

SAVOY CABBAGE AND STILTON SOUP

171 calories

Serves 4 • Ready in 40 minutes

1 tsp olive oil (27 cals)

2 leeks, trimmed and sliced (53 cals)

1 potato (170g/6oz), peeled and diced (128 cals)

500ml (generous 2 cups) vegetable stock, fresh or made with ½ cube (18 cals)

¼ Savoy cabbage (100g/3½oz), outer leaves removed and shredded (27 cals)

2 tbsp sherry (28 cals)

50g (1¾oz) Stilton, crumbled (205 cals)

200ml (generous ¾ cup) skimmed milk (64 cals)

2 tbsp double cream (135 cals)

salt and freshly ground black pepper

- Heat the oil in a large saucepan and gently fry the leeks for 10 minutes until tender.
- Stir in the potato and add the stock. Bring to the boil, then reduce the heat and simmer gently for 15 minutes. Use a potato masher in the soup to mash the potatoes until smooth (or blend in a blender if you prefer).
- Add the cabbage and sherry. Bring to a gentle simmer and cook for 5 minutes until the cabbage is tender. Stir in the stilton, milk and cream and heat until the stilton has melted. Season well before serving.

SLOW ONION SOUP

197 calories

You need to cook the onions long and slow to get that beautiful onion sweetness.

Serves 4 • Ready in 1hr 45mins

1 tbsp olive oil (99 cals)

15g (1 tbsp) butter (112 cals)

1kg (2lb 2 oz) onions, peeled and finely sliced (360 cals)

1 garlic clove, peeled and finely sliced (3 cals)

2 fresh thyme leaves, finely chopped (or 1 tsp dried thyme)

1 bay leaf

salt and freshly ground black pepper

150ml (generous ½ cup) red wine (129 cals)

1 litre (generous 4 cups) beef stock (fresh is really good here, but you can use 2 cubes) (70 cals)

1 tsp caster sugar (16 cals)

- Heat the oil and butter gently in a wide lidded frying pan. When the butter has melted, add the onions, garlic, thyme and bay leaf. Season generously with salt and pepper and stir.
- With the heat on the lowest possible setting, put the lid on the pan and cook for about 1 hour, stirring occasionally.
- Add the wine, stock and sugar, then bring to the boil, reduce the heat and simmer for 30 minutes before serving.

MUSHROOM AND BACON SOUP

184 calories (105 calories without bacon and extra mushrooms)

This winter warmer can of course be made without the bacon and extra mushrooms. I find adding the bacon makes it into a "proper" meal. This soup can be frozen in individual portions.

Serves 4 • Ready in 45 minutes

1 tsp olive oil (27 cals)

1 medium onion, peeled and roughly chopped (65 cals)

2 cloves garlic, peeled and chopped (8 cals)

1 parsnip, peeled and roughly chopped (45 cals)

1 medium potato, peeled and roughly chopped (135 cals)

1 carrot, peeled & chopped (35 cals)

salt and pepper to taste

250g (9oz) mushrooms, washed & sliced (32)

5 dried porcini mushrooms (5 cals)

1 tsp mushroom ketchup/soy sauce (2)

200ml (generous ¾ cup) dry white wine (66 cals)

1 litre water

To serve (per person):

2 slices streaky bacon (66 cals)

100g (3½oz) mushrooms, washed & sliced (13cals)

sprig fresh parsley, chopped (optional)

- Place the porcini mushrooms in a cup and add about half a cup of boiling water. Leave to soak for at least 10 minutes.
- Heat the olive oil gently in a large lidded saucepan or casserole dish. Add the onion, stir and replace the lid. Cook for 5 minutes.

- Add the garlic, parsnip, potato and carrot. Season generously with salt and pepper. Stir, replace the lid and sweat the vegetables for a further 5 minutes. Remove the lid from the pan. Add the mushrooms and stir in.
- Remove the porcini mushrooms from their soaking liquor, roughly chop and add to the pan. Pour most of the soaking liquor into the pan, discarding the dregs at the bottom. Finally add the mushroom ketchup, white wine and approximately 1 litre of water. Bring to the boil and simmer gently for 30 minutes.
- Transfer the soup (in 2 batches if necessary) to a liquidiser or blender. Blend until smooth. Return to the pan and re-heat. If you are saving or freezing some of the soup, now is the time to transfer to containers.
- When you are ready to serve the soup, heat a small non-stick frying pan on med-high. When hot, add the bacon slices and fry for about 2 minutes each side until crunchy and browned. Remove the bacon to kitchen paper and dab on all sides to remove excess fat.
- Into the same hot frying pan add the mushrooms. They will take on board the bacon fat as they fry. Cook for 3-4 minutes, stirring regularly, until glossy and brown.
- Serve the warmed soup in a wide bowl, with the mushrooms piled in the middle and the bacon laid over the top with a little fresh parsley.

SPRING CHICKEN STEW

365 calories

This is a pleasing and quick chicken stew.

Serves 2 • Ready in 1 hour

50g (¼ cup) chopped streaky bacon or lardons (138 cals)

2 skinless, boneless chicken thighs, about 360g (12oz) (392 cals)

½ leek, trimmed and roughly chopped (13 cals)

1 celery stick, finely sliced (2 cals)

2 garlic cloves, peeled and finely sliced (6 cals)

1 tsp mixed dried herbs (8 cals)

200ml (generous ¾ cup) dry (hard) cider (72 cals)

80g (¾ cup) frozen peas (53 cals)

1 tbsp Dijon mustard (28 cals)

salt and freshly ground black pepper

1 Little Gem (Boston) lettuce, roughly shredded (17 cals)

fresh tarragon (optional)

- Heat the chopped bacon or lardons in a heavy-based lidded saucepan, cooking them until they brown all over. Remove them from the pan with a slotted spoon and set aside. Add the chicken thighs and cook on the first side for about 5 minutes over a medium heat.
- Turn the chicken over and add the leek, celery, garlic and dried herbs. Give everything a stir and let it continue to cook for a further 5 minutes. Return the chopped bacon or lardons to the pan.
- Pour in the cider and add the peas. Bring to the boil, then reduce the heat, put the lid on and cook for 20–30 minutes until the chicken is cooked through.

- Remove the lid, stir in the mustard and season with salt and pepper. Finally, toss the lettuce and tarragon over the chicken and let it wilt into the sauce for about 2 minutes.
- Serve immediately.

RED PEPPER AND GOAT'S CHEESE SOUP

229 calories

This soup combines sweet and salty flavours to make an unusual and satisfying soup.

Serves 4 • Ready in 45 mins

1 tsp olive oil (27 cals)

1 onion, roughly chopped (65 cals)

50g (1¾oz) red lentils (159 cals)

1 litre vegetable stock, made with 2 stock cubes (70 cals)

200ml white wine (66 cals)

4 red peppers, de-seeded and roughly chopped (204 cals)

1 apple, peeled, cored and chopped (47 cals)

2 tsp dried basil

80g rindless goat's cheese, roughly cut or broken up (278 cals)

- Heat the olive oil gently in a large saucepan and fry the onions for 5 minutes. Add the lentils, stir and pour in half the stock. Bring to the boil and simmer vigorously for 10 minutes. Then add the red peppers, apple, basil, white wine and the rest of the stock. Bring back to a gentle simmer and cook for a further 30 minutes.
- Transfer to a blender, you'll need to do this in two or more batches, and blend until smooth. Return the soup to the pan and reheat gently. Stir in the goat's cheese until melted, then serve.

HAM, LENTIL AND PEARL BARLEY SOUP

221 calories

Two types of lentils plus the pearl barley make this a great recipe for a healthy heart.

Serves 4 • Ready in 2 hours

1 tbsp olive oil (99 cals)

1 onion, finely diced (65 cals)

2 carrots, diced (70 cals)

30g red lentils (95 cals)

30g green puy lentils (89 cals)

30g pearl barley (108 cals)

750ml chicken stock, fresh or made with 1½ stock cubes (53 cals)

250g cooked ham or gammon, cut into bite sized pieces (230 cals)

1 small potato (100g), peeled and diced (75 cals)

- Heat the oil in a large saucepan or casserole and fry the onions and carrots very gently for 10 minutes until the onions are transparent.
- Rinse the lentils and pearl barley, stir into the pan and then add the stock. Bring to the boil, cover and simmer for 45 minutes.
- Add the ham and potato and simmer for a further 30 minutes.

Healthy Diet Recipes

VEGETARIAN

Fresh, Healthy and Easy Recipes
from best-selling cookery author,
Jacqueline Whitehart.

Healthy Diet Recipes: Vegetarian

Healthy Diet Recipes: Vegetarian

This new set of easy diet recipes are designed to be easy to follow, quick recipes that you can with little fuss. I love cooking for myself and my family but often find that cookbooks tend towards the 'special' or 'weekend' recipes whereas what we want 99% of the time is something simple and healthy that we can make from scratch and avoid the dreaded processed or ready meals. All the recipes are carefully created to be well-balanced and healthy and are calorie-counted for your convenience. Most if not all recipes can be kept or frozen in individual portions to provide several days' worth of healthy meals.

A lot of diet vegetarian dishes are low in filling protein and fats. This book tries to re-dress the balance by providing substantial but still low calorie dishes. You won't go hungry here.

CHEESY HERB MUFFINS

131 calories per muffin

These muffins are great for breakfast or as a light snack.

Serves 12 • Ready in 30 minutes

180ml skimmed milk (58 cals)

juice of ½ lemon (2 cals)

80g frozen spinach (18 cals)

100g plain (all-purpose) flour (341 cals)

100g wholemeal self-raising (wholewheat self-rising) flour (310 cals)

small handful of chives, finely chopped (2 cals)

small handful of fresh parsley, finely chopped (3 cals)

40g (1½oz) Parmesan cheese, finely grated (181 cals)

½ tsp bicarbonate of soda

2 tsp baking powder (14 cals)

pinch of salt

1 large egg (91 cals)

75g butter, melted (558 cals)

- Pre-heat the oven to 200C/180C fan/400F. Line a 12-hole cake tin with paper cases.
- Combine the milk and lemon juice in a bowl or jug and leave to rest for 5 minutes.
- Reheat the spinach in the microwave for about 1 minute, then squeeze out any water.
- Mix the flours, herbs, cheese, bicarbonate of soda, baking powder and salt together in a large bowl, then stir in the spinach.
- In another bowl, whisk the egg and melted butter together, then add the curdled milk.

- Pour the liquid ingredients over the dry ingredients and stir together. Do not overmix, it should stay rather lumpy.
- Spoon a fat teaspoon of batter into each paper case and bake in the oven for 20–25 minutes until just browning on top. Remove from the oven and leave to cool in the tin.
- These are equally good hot or cold.

MUSHROOM STIR-FRY

146 calories

This is a filling and substantial stir-fry, yet it is low in calories too.

Serves 1 • Ready in 10 minutes

½ tsp walnut oil (20 cals)

1 tbsp dark soy sauce (6 cals)

1 tsp soft dark brown sugar (18 cals)

½ tsp sunflower oil (14 cals)

½ garlic clove, peeled and finely chopped (2 cals)

½ yellow (bell) pepper, deseeded and cut into thin slices (21 cals)

½ small carrot, peeled and cut into very thin sticks (14 cals)

1 small thumb fresh root ginger, peeled and cut into very thin sticks (6 cals)

50g (1¾oz) beansprouts (16 cals)

50g (1¾oz) mangetout (16 cals)

100g (3½oz) mushrooms, sliced (13 cals)

- In a bowl, mix together the walnut oil, soy sauce and brown sugar to make a sauce.
- Heat the oil in a wok or large frying pan over a high heat, toss in the garlic, pepper, carrot and ginger and stir-fry for 2 minutes. Add the beansprouts, mange tout and mushrooms and stir-fry for a further 2 minutes. Reduce the heat to medium, add the sauce and cook for another 2 minutes. Serve immediately.

SPICY BEAN BURGERS

202 calories per burger

These burgers are a great standby. Quick to prepare and cook.

MAKES 4 BURGERS • *Ready in 20 minutes*

1×400g (14oz) can cannellini beans, rinsed and drained (259 cals)

2 tbsp (50g/1¾oz) red pesto (164 cals)

75g (3oz) wholemeal breadcrumbs (163 cals)

1 large egg (91 cals)

4 spring onions (scallions), trimmed and chopped (20 cals)

1 garlic clove, peeled and crushed (4 cals)

salt and freshly ground black pepper

4 tsp sunflower oil (1 tsp per burger) (108 cals)

- Use a potato masher to thoroughly mash the beans. Add the pesto, breadcrumbs, egg, spring onions and crushed garlic. Add a little salt and pepper and mix well.
- Divide the mixture into 4 portions and form into balls. Place on a baking tray or plate. Squeeze the ball down with the palm of your hand to form a burger. The burgers can be chilled at this stage and will keep refrigerated for 2 days.
- When you are ready to cook the burgers, heat the oil in a frying pan (skillet) over a medium heat. Add the burgers to the pan and cook for 4–5 minutes on each side until golden. Serve hot.

FRESH SAAG PANEER

176 calories per serving

Using fresh spinach in this recipe gives the dish more zing. If you can't get paneer, try queso blanco instead.

SERVES 4 • *Ready in 45 minutes*

1 tbsp rice bran oil (99 cals)

250g (9oz) paneer, cut into cubes (425 cals)

1 onion, chopped (65 cals)

1 thumb-sized piece of ginger, peeled and cut into matchsticks (10 cals)

2 cloves garlic, finely sliced (8 cals)

1 fresh green chilli, seeded and cut into rings (2 cals)

1 tsp tomato purée (8 cals)

200g (7oz) cherry tomatoes, halved (38 cals)

1 tsp ground coriander

1 tsp ground cumin

¼ tsp ground turmeric

1 tsp mild chilli powder

200g (7oz) fresh spinach leaves (48 cals)

Salt and freshly ground black pepper

- Heat the oil in a wide, lidded frying pan over a high heat. Add the paneer cubes and season generously. Fry for a few minutes until golden, stirring often. Remove from the pan and set aside.
- Reduce the heat and add the onion. Fry for 5 minutes before adding the ginger, garlic and chilli. Fry for another 5 minutes. Add the tomato purée and cherry tomatoes. Put the lid on the pan and cook for a further 5–7 minutes.
- Add all the spices and a little more salt. Return the paneer to the pan and stir until coated. Then add the spinach leaves and return the lid to the pan. Allow the spinach to wilt for 2–3 minutes and then stir into the sauce.

RED DAL CURRY

196 calories per serving

This filling dish freezes really well, so make a big pot and freeze some for a speedy dinner another day.

SERVES 4 • *Ready in 1 hour*

1 tbsp sunflower oil (99 cals)

1 large onion, peeled and finely chopped (86 cals)

4 garlic cloves, peeled and finely chopped (12 cals)

thumb-sized piece fresh root ginger, peeled and grated (5 cals)

1 large red chilli, deseeded and chopped into fine rings (3 cals)

¼ tsp ground turmeric

¼ tsp cayenne pepper

1 tsp paprika (7 cals)

½ tsp ground cumin

a pinch of salt

180g (6oz) dried red lentils, rinsed (572 cals)

juice of 2 limes (7 cals)

1 tomato, finely chopped (14 cals)

- Heat the oil in a heavy-based pan over a low-medium heat. Add the onion, garlic, ginger and chilli and stir-fry for 3–4 minutes. Add the ground spices and salt and stir-fry for another minute. Add the lentils, stir, then pour in 900ml (3½ cups) water and bring to the boil.
- Reduce the heat slightly and simmer vigorously for 10 mins, then reduce the heat to low and cook for a further 35–40 mins, stirring regularly, until all the water has been absorbed. If the dal is too thick or starts to stick, just add a little more water.
- When the dal has the consistency of thick porridge, add the lime juice and tomato and cook for a further 3 minutes before serving.

VEGGIE CHILLI

184 calories per serving

Satisfying and filling chilli. Serve with a small portion of brown rice if desired. This chilli freezes well so make a batch and keep it in the freezer for home-made ready meals.

SERVES 6 • *Ready in 1 hour*

800g (1lb 12oz) butternut squash (1 medium), peeled, seeded and cut into small chunks (288 cals)

½ tsp cinnamon

salt and pepper

1 tbsp plus 1 tsp olive oil (126 cals)

1 onion, chopped (65 cals)

1 green pepper, seeded and chopped (24 cals)

2 fresh red or green chillies, seeded and sliced into rings (8 cals)

2 cloves garlic, finely chopped (8 cals)

zest and juice of 1 lime (4 cals)

2 tsp mild chilli powder

2 tsp ground cumin

1 tsp paprika (14 cals)

1 tsp cocoa powder (16 cals)

2×400g (14oz) tins chopped tomatoes (128 cals)

2×400g (14oz) tins kidney beans, rinsed and drained (420 cals)

Salt and freshly ground black pepper

- Preheat the oven to 220C/200C fan/425F.
- Place the butternut squash on a baking tray, sprinkle over the cinnamon and season generously with salt and pepper. Drizzle over 1 tablespoon of olive oil and toss through with your hands. Bake in

the oven for 15–20 minutes, until just tender.

- Meanwhile, heat the remaining teaspoon of olive oil in a large pan and add the onion, green pepper and chillies. Fry gently for 5 minutes. Add the garlic and lime zest and cook for a further minute or two. Add the cumin, paprika and cocoa powder. Stir through before adding the chopped tomatoes and kidney beans.
- Bring up to a gentle simmer and cook, lid off, for about 30 minutes. Add the butternut squash and lime juice and stir through gently. Taste and adjust the seasoning and cook for a further 5 minutes before serving.
- The chilli keeps well in the fridge or can be made in advance and frozen.

COURGETTE 'PIZZA' BITES

216 calories

This dish is such an easy guilt-free treat.

SERVES 1 • *Ready in 10 minutes*

2 medium courgettes (zucchini) (54 cals)

2 tsp garlic oil (54 cals)

salt and freshly ground black pepper

2 medium tomatoes, finely chopped (28 cals)

50g (1¾oz) low-fat mozzarella, chopped (80 cals)

4 fresh basil leaves

- Preheat the grill to a high setting.
- Cut the courgettes (zucchini) in half on the diagonal so you get 2 oval slices (about 1cm/ ½ inch thick) from each courgette (zucchini).
- Put the garlic oil in a small bowl. Crumple up a piece of kitchen paper (paper towel), dip it into the oil and rub the courgette (zucchini) slices on both sides with the oil.
- Lay out the courgettes (zucchini) on a grill (broiler) pan and cook under the grill for 2 minutes on each side.
- Remove from the grill and distribute the chopped tomatoes over each slice of courgette (zucchini).
- Next, top with the mozzarella and finally a basil leaf.
- Return to the grill and cook until the cheese starts to bubble.

ROASTED RED PEPPER COUSCOUS

216 calories

Prepare this salad a little differently, by dressing the couscous before it's rehydrated. You also 'cook' the couscous in cold water so it retains a satisfying bite.

SERVES 1 • *Ready in 30 minutes*

1 red pepper, whole (51 cals)

1 tsp extra-virgin olive oil (27 cals)

½ tsp English mustard (6 cals)

1 tbsp white wine vinegar (1 cal)

½ tsp granulated sugar (8 cals)

salt and freshly ground black pepper

1 tsp chopped fresh coriander (cilantro) leaves

1 tsp chopped fresh basil leaves

40g (1½oz) couscous, uncooked (91 cals)

10 cherry tomatoes, cut into quarters (22 cals)

100g (3½oz) cucumber, peeled & diced (10 cals)

- Preheat the oven to 200C/fan 180C/400F.
- Place the red pepper on a baking sheet and roast in the oven for 20 minutes.
- Meanwhile, make a dressing by mixing the olive oil, mustard, vinegar, sugar, salt and pepper and herbs together in a small bowl.
- Place the couscous in a bowl, then pour over the dressing and mix lightly with a fork. Leave to stand for 5 minutes, then pour over enough water just to cover the couscous and leave for a further 15 minutes until the couscous has absorbed the water. Fluff the couscous up with a fork.
- When the pepper is cooked, take out of the oven and remove and discard the stalk and seeds. Remove any loose pieces of skin, then chop the pepper flesh into cubes and add to the couscous together with the tomatoes and cucumber. Serve immediately or keep in the refrigerator for up to two days.

LENTIL AND MUSHROOM BOLOGNAISE

220 calories per serving

This bolognaise is so filling and versatile that you simply don't need the meat. There is enough here to serve 6 but it freezes well so you can freeze individual portions. Simply re-heat in the microwave for a delicious meal in seconds.

SERVES 6 • Ready in 1hr 10 mins

1 tbsp olive oil (99 cals)

1 large onion, chopped (79 cals)

250g (9oz) mushrooms, washed and sliced (40 cals)

4 cloves garlic, sliced (16 cals)

1 carrot, peeled and chopped (35 cals)

1 green (bell) pepper, seeded and chopped (21 cals)

250g (9oz) brown or green lentils (795 cals)

1×400g (14oz) tin chopped tomatoes (64 cals)

1 bay leaf

500ml (generous 2 cups) vegetable stock, fresh or made with 1 stock cube (35 cals)

½ tsp chilli flakes

200ml red wine (136 cals)

- In a large pan, heat the oil over a medium heat. Fry the onion for 5 minutes. Add the mushrooms, garlic, carrot and green pepper. Cook for 15–20 minutes until soft, stirring frequently.
- Stir in the lentils, then add the chopped tomatoes, bay leaf, vegetable stock and chilli flakes. Bring to the boil and cook on a vigorous heat for 10 minutes. Reduce the heat to medium/low, add the wine and cook for a further 20–30 minutes until the sauce is rich and thick.

LEEK SWIRLS WITH OLIVES AND WATERCRESS

233 calories

Hearty, warming and filling, what's not to like?

SERVES 1 • *Ready in 15 minutes*

1 tsp olive oil (27 cals)

2 leeks, trimmed and cut into 1cm wide slices (52 cals)

zest of 1 lemon

juice of ½ lemon (2 cals)

1 tsp extra virgin olive oil (27 cals)

salt and freshly ground black pepper

10g (1/3oz) parmesan, fresh grated (83 cals)

50g (1¾oz) watercress or baby spinach leaves (11 cals)

6 black olives, pitted (31 cals)

- In a wide lidded pan, heat the olive oil over a medium-high heat. When hot, add the leeks and stir-fry for 2 minutes. Reduce the heat, add about 2 tablespoons water and put the lid on. Steam until tender, about 10 minutes.
- Combine the lemon zest, lemon juice, extra virgin olive oil, salt and pepper and half the parmesan in a small bowl.
- Stir the watercress, olives and lemon dressing through the leek swirls.
- Transfer to a serving bowl and sprinkle on the remaining parmesan. Season generously with salt and pepper and serve.

COURGETTE AND FETA FRITTERS

260 calories per serving

SERVES 2 • *Ready in 20 minutes*

2 courgettes (zucchini), trimmed (54 cals)

3 spring onions (scallions), trimmed and finely chopped (15 cals)

100g (3½oz) light feta cheese, crumbled (182 cals)

little fresh parsley, chopped (2 cals)

1 tsp dried mint (6 cals)

½ tsp paprika (3 cals)

salt and freshly ground black pepper

1 level tbsp plain flour (68 cals)

1 large egg, beaten (91 cals)

1 tbsp olive oil (99 cals)

- Coarsely grate the courgettes (zucchini) and lay out on kitchen paper to dry out. Leave for about 10 minutes, then pat the top of the courgette to remove excess moisture.
- Mix the spring onions, crumbled feta, parsley, mint and paprika in a bowl. Season with salt and pepper and stir in the flour. Pour in the beaten egg and mix well. Finally, mix in the grated courgette (zucchini).
- Heat the oil in a wide frying pan over a medium-high heat. When hot, add 1 tablespoon scoops of the mixture to the pan, flattening each scoop with the back of the spoon as you go.
- The fritters need to be widely spaced so you may have to do this in 2 batches. Fry for about 2 minutes on each side until golden. Serve immediately.

THAI VEGETABLE CURRY

238 calories per serving

This quick to cook yet filling and warming Thai curry is a joy on a cold winter's day.

SERVES 2 • *Ready in 10 minutes*

1 tsp sesame oil (27 cals)

½ tsp garlic oil (14 cals)

2 spring onions (scallions), chopped (12 cals)

1 thumb-sized piece ginger, peeled and cut into matchsticks (10 cals)

1 red (bell) pepper, de-seeded and finely chopped (51 cals)

1 green chilli, de-seeded and chopped (4 cals)

250g mushrooms, washed and sliced (40 cals)

80g spinach, fresh or frozen (17 cals)

1 can (400ml) light coconut milk (292 cals)

2 fresh basil leaves, chopped

generous handful fresh coriander, chopped

juice of 1 lime (4 cals)

- Heat the sesame and garlic-infused oil in a deep frying pan. Add the spring onions (scallions), ginger, red pepper and green chilli and stir-fry for 2 minutes. Turn the heat to high, add the mushrooms and fry, stirring frequently until tender and glossy.
- If you are using frozen spinach, add it now. Then add the coconut milk. Simmer gently for 5 minutes.
- Turn the heat off and stir in the basil, coriander and fresh spinach (if using). Squeeze in the lime juice and serve.

PATATAS BRAVAS

248 calories

This is my take on the classic Spanish dish.

SERVES 1 • *Ready in 25 minutes*

180g (6oz) new potatoes (about 4 small), with skin on (126 cals)

salt and freshly ground black pepper

1 tsp olive oil (27 cals)

1 shallot, peeled and diced (6 cals)

1 garlic clove, peeled and sliced (3 cals)

1 red chilli, finely chopped (3 cals)

1 tbsp tomato purée (30 cals)

pinch of sugar

¼ tsp smoked paprika (2 cals)

10 ripe cherry tomatoes, halved (22 cals)

1 tbsp red wine vinegar (2 cals)

1 tsp rapeseed oil (27 cals)

- Quarter the new potatoes and place in a saucepan of cold salted water. Bring the pan to the boil and cook until tender. This will take 12–15 minutes from cold. When cooked, drain the potatoes and lay on kitchen paper (paper towels) to cool and dry.
- Heat the olive oil in a frying pan over a medium heat. Add the shallot and cook for 5 minutes before adding the garlic and red chilli and frying for another 2 minutes.
- Stir in the tomato purée, a pinch of salt, the sugar and paprika and fry for 1 minute before tossing in the tomatoes and vinegar. Cook gently for 10–15 minutes until thick. If it starts to stick to the pan add a little water to loosen the sauce.
- When the potatoes are cool, heat the rapeseed oil in a wide pan over a high heat. When hot, add the potatoes and stir once. Leave to fry

until golden on one side, do not stir, this will take about 3 minutes. Turn the potatoes and fry for a further 3 minutes until crispy and brown all over.

- Loosely stir the potatoes into the sauce and serve immediately with a generous sprinkling of black pepper.

MOROCCAN VEGETABLE TAGINE

262 calories

This dish is unusual and very filling.

SERVES 2 • *Ready in 45 minutes*

1 tsp olive oil (27 cals)

1 onion, peeled and chopped (54 cals)

1 garlic clove, peeled and finely chopped (3 cals)

2 tsp ground cumin

¼ tsp ground cinnamon

2 tsp ground coriander

1 tbsp tomato purée (paste) (30 cals)

1 tsp harissa paste (4 cals)

½ red pepper, de-seeded and diced (27 cals)

1 × 200g (7oz) can chickpeas (or half 400g/14oz can), rinsed and drained (138 cals)

40g (1½oz) red lentils (dry weight), rinsed (127 cals)

1 potato (170g/6oz), peeled and diced (75 cals)

500ml (generous 2 cups) vegetable stock (fresh or made with 1 cube) (35 cals)

juice of 1 lemon (3 cals)

- Heat the oil in a large saucepan, add the onion and fry for 7–8 minutes until translucent. Add the garlic and fry for 1 more minute. Stir in the spices, tomato puree (paste) and harissa paste, then add the diced pepper and fry for 3 minutes.
- Add the chickpeas, lentils, potato, stock and lemon juice. Bring to the boil, reduce the heat slightly and simmer vigorously for 10 minutes, before reducing the heat and simmering gently for a further 15 minutes.

NORTH AFRICAN HALLOUMI

267 calories per serving

There's a touch of heat to this dish, tempered by the sweetness of the butternut squash and the saltiness of the halloumi.

SERVES 2 • *Ready in 15 minutes*

300g/11oz (½ small) butternut squash, peeled and cut into large chunks (108 cals)

1 tsp cumin seeds

1 tsp chilli flakes

1 tsp rapeseed oil (27 cals)

2 tsp tomato purée (8 cals)

1 tsp garlic purée (or 1 clove, crushed) (8 cals)

100g (3½oz) halloumi, cut into chunks (315 cals)

1 spring onion (scallion), trimmed and chopped (6 cals)

50g (1¾oz) piquante peppers from a jar, drained and chopped (57 cals)

Juice of 1 lime (4 cals)

Freshly ground black pepper

Handful of fresh coriander (cilantro), chopped (optional)

- Place the cubed butternut squash into a microwave safe dish, cover and microwave for 5 minutes on high.
- Place a frying pan over a medium/high heat and toss in the cumin seeds and chilli flakes. Dry fry for one minute, then reduce the heat to medium and add the oil, tomato purée and garlic. Stir for a few seconds before adding the halloumi and spring onions. Stir-fry for 3 minutes.
- Add the peppers and butternut squash and continue to cook, stirring regularly, until browned on all sides. Remove from the heat and stir in the lime juice, black pepper and coriander. Serve immediately.

PUY LENTIL AND FETA SALAD

273 calories per serving

This is an easy salad that you can put together using store cupboard ingredients.

SERVES 2 • *Ready in 10 minutes*

For the dressing:

1 tbsp balsamic vinegar (15 cals)

1 tsp walnut oil (27 cals)

2 tsp extra-virgin olive oil (54 cals)

½ tsp English mustard (6 cals)

Salt and freshly ground pepper

For the salad:

1×400g (14oz) can ready-to-eat puy lentils, drained (172 cals)

30g (1oz) roasted red peppers from a tin or jar, drained and chopped (7 cals)

30g (1oz) rocket leaves (10 cals)

6 cherry tomatoes, halved (27 cals)

50g (1¾oz) light feta cheese, cut into rough cubes (90 cals)

20g (¾oz) walnuts, halved (137 cals)

- Prepare the dressing by mixing together the balsamic vinegar, walnut oil, olive oil, English mustard and salt and pepper.
- In a large bowl combine the lentils with the roasted red peppers, rocket leaves and cherry tomatoes. Stir about three-quarters of the dressing through. Arrange the feta and walnuts over the top and finally drizzle over the rest of the dressing.

RATATOUILLE BAKE

274 calories per serving

SERVES 2 • *Ready in 50 minutes*

300g (11oz) new potatoes, skin on (210 cals)

1 medium aubergine/eggplant (300g/11oz) (45 cals)

2 courgettes (zucchini) (54 cals)

2 tsp olive oil (54 cals)

1 onion chopped (65 cals)

1 clove garlic, chopped (4 cals)

1 red pepper, seeded & chopped (51 cals)

1×400g (14oz) can chopped tomatoes (64 cals)

fresh basil, chopped

- Boil or steam the potatoes until just tender. Allow to cool completely before cutting into thin slices. Preheat the oven to 200C/180C fan/400F.
- Wash and slice the aubergine (eggplant) and courgette (zucchini) into slices about ½cm thick. Quarter the aubergine (eggplant) slices.
- In a saucepan heat the olive oil and gently fry the onion and garlic for about 5 minutes. Add the chopped pepper and the aubergine (eggplant) and courgettes (zucchini). Add the basil and season generously with salt and pepper. Put the lid on and turn the heat to low and cook for 20 minutes. Pour over the chopped tomatoes and bring up to a gentle simmer for 5 minutes.
- Transfer to a small baking dish. Place one layer of the sliced potatoes over the top of the dish and press lightly into the sauce. Arrange the rest of the potatoes over the top. Bake in the oven for 20 minutes or until the potatoes are brown and crunchy.

AUTUMN VEGETABLE CRUMBLE

327 calories per serving

This is a super healthy and filling vegetarian meal.

SERVES 4 • *Ready in 1hr 30 mins*

2 tbsp olive oil (198 cals)

1 large onion, peeled and chopped (86 cals)

2 garlic cloves, peeled and sliced (6 cals)

1 red chilli, deseeded and chopped (3 cals)

1×400g (14oz) can chopped tomatoes (64 cals)

300ml (generous 1 cup) white wine (198 cals)

500ml (2 cups) vegetable stock (35 cals)

1 bay leaf

2 fresh thyme sprigs (or ½ tsp dried)

600g (1lb 5oz) butternut squash (about 1 large), peeled, de-seeded and cut into chunks (216 cals)

1×400g (14oz) can butterbeans, rinsed and drained (220 cals)

50g (1¾oz) wholemeal breadcrumbs (108 cals)

5g (1 tsp) Parmesan, grated (21 cals)

25g (1oz) chopped nuts (152 cals)

handful of fresh parsley, chopped (3 cals)

Salt and freshly ground black pepper

- Heat 1 tablespoon of oil in a large pan, add the onion and fry gently for 8 minutes. Add the garlic and chilli and fry for a further 2 minutes.
- Stir in the chopped tomatoes, white wine, vegetable stock, bay leaf and thyme. Bring to the boil, then reduce the heat to medium–low and simmer, uncovered, for 20 minutes.

- Add the butternut squash and cook for a further 20 minutes. Stir in the butter beans.
- Preheat the oven 180C/160C fan/350F.
- Mix the breadcrumbs, Parmesan, chopped nuts, parsley and the remaining tablespoon of oil together.
- Transfer the vegetable sauce to a suitable casserole dish and sprinkle on the crumble topping. Season liberally with salt and pepper. Bake in the oven for 30 minutes or until the crumble is golden and crisp.

BAKED MUSHROOM AND BLUE CHEESE RISOTTO

304 calories per serving

Baking the risotto in the oven makes this dish easy peasy.

SERVES 2 • *Ready in 1 hour*

1 tsp olive oil (27 cals)

1 red onion, peeled and chopped (54 cals)

200g (7oz) mushrooms, sliced (26 cals)

100g (3½oz) brown rice, rinsed (357 cals)

300ml (generous 1 cup) vegetable stock (fresh or made with ½ cube) (18 cals)

juice of ½ lemon (2 cals)

30g (1oz) blue cheese, crumbled (123 cals)

salt and freshly ground black pepper

- Preheat the oven to 200C/180C fan/400F.
- Heat the oil in an oven-proof casserole, add the onion and fry for 3 minutes. Toss in the mushrooms and fry for a further 2 minutes.
- Tip in the rice and stir through. Add the stock and bring to a gentle simmer.
- Cover with a lid and place in the oven. Cook for 45–55 minutes (reduce this to 20 minutes if you are using white rice), checking if you need to add more water halfway through, until the rice is tender.
- Stir through the lemon juice and blue cheese. Season to taste before serving.

Index

Printed in Great Britain
by Amazon